Flourishing Finances

Teaching "Bloomanistas" Financial Responsibility

Gerlisa D. Shipman

TTL Publishing

WAKE FOREST, NORTH CAROLINA

Flourishing Finances by Gerlisa D. Shipman
TTL Publishing
P.O. Box 1744
Wake Forest, North Carolina 27588
info@tokunbotheleader.com
Visit the publisher's website at tokunbotheleader.com.

Visit the author's website at bloomanista.org.

Unless otherwise noted, all scriptures are taken from the New Living Translation Bible.

Flourishing Finances/Gerlisa D. Shipman
ISBN: 978-1-7378576-5-5

Contents

Introduction

Money is a hot topic in our society. As a future entrepreneur, writer, politician, artist, wife, and mother, how you manage your money will play a key role in your success. There are many strategies, books, and ideas that give you principles around money. Unfortunately, many of these resources do not involve the One who allowed there to be wealth, Jesus Christ! One of my favorite scriptures in the Bible is Galatians 5:25 (NLT) which states, “Since we are living by the spirit, let us follow the Spirit's leading in every part of our lives.” The Holy Spirit will not only lead you in your decisions around relationships and career paths, but He will also guide you in making quality financial decisions.

When I was a sophomore in college, I had a traumatic experience of being homeless. My parents both lost their jobs and foreclosed on the home where I housed all of my childhood memories. Thankfully, I was able to stay with my closest childhood friend, and my parents were able to stay with other family members. While I was sharing a bed with my best friend and living in the corner of her room, I realized that I had to learn how to be financially free from my parents. This devastating moment made me realize that it was time for me to start taking responsibility for my finances bit by bit. The harsh reality was that no one in my family managed money effectively, nor were they able to counsel me to help me get to the level of wealth that I am called to have in my purpose. Being homeless forced me to think differently about money. The more I grew in my relationship with Christ, the more I realized how God wanted to be Lord over my finances. Being Lord over my finances meant that He wanted me to rely on Him to help me have a godly and wise perspective of wealth. I realized that I was floundering financially because I depended on myself to manage the money that was given to me. There were too many times when I let my emotions, lustful desires, and lack of self-control dominate my choices on money. When I began to allow God to lead me in this area, I learned that I was inviting His wisdom into my life. Soon, I understood that where His wisdom is, abundant life was also there. As a result, my finances began to tremendously flourish.

As the CEO and Founder of Efflorescence Girls, LLC, my assignment is to provide you with a godly perspective on, identity, relationships, mental health, self-love, life goals, and financial literacy. For this book, my vision is to see you flourish in your finances by establishing a godly perspective on money. This book was written to share with you the toughest lessons I learned about money, the wisdom I've gained from God about finances, and the practical steps I use to handle money. As we journey together in this area of your life, I believe God will pour His wisdom into you so that you may flourish in your finances and become a "Bloomanista!" A Bloom-a-nista is a term that my step-sister and I came up with. The term, Bloomanista, is used to describe young adult women who are dedicated to becoming a better version of themselves. Bloominstas are committed to learning and growing so that they can be all that God has created them to be, especially in the area of finances.

You are reading this because you are interested in becoming the best version of yourself. Allow this book to help you evolve by stretching your belief systems about money. Use this book as one of your tools to help you flourish in your finances.

One

Flourishing in Identity

In order to see God move in your finances, it's imperative to understand your identity, purpose, talents, goals, dreams, and the tithing principle. These six areas will help you have order and control in your finances. They will also be an essential part of helping you create your budget. In this chapter, you will dive deep into why each of these six concepts is a crucial part of seeing your finances flourish.

God-Given Identity

Knowing your identity in Christ is a vital piece of understanding God's perspective on how you manage your money. Over the last two decades of my life, I've spent time allowing God to secure my identity. The process of understanding who I am in Christ has had many ups and downs. It has been filled with many tears, losses, journal entries, unlearning, investigating, counseling sessions, and so much more. If I'm completely honest, I am still letting God reshape my identity in various ways. The more that I allowed God to change my erroneous perspective of myself and secure my identity in Him, the more lively and free I became. There were parts of my identity that were awakened once I allowed Him to reshape my thinking about who I am in His eyes. Ephesians 1, states the definition of identity. The Bible describes that before God made the world, God loved us and chose us in Christ to be holy and without fault in His eyes. When we became believers, we became adopted daughters into the royal family of Jesus Christ. Through His blood that He shed on Calvary, we received an inheritance! His blood washed away our sins, freed us from any shame, demonic oppression, guilty consciences, and it made us anew. The best part of being a daughter of the Most-High God is that there is nothing that we could ever do to separate us from the love of Jesus.

Furthermore, too many of us build our identity on how much money we have or do not have in our bank accounts. God wants us to have a solid identity in Him so that we do not turn money into being our god. He wants us to control money, He does not want money to control us and how we feel about ourselves. Learning our value in Christ causes us to have a better relationship with money. We make better financial decisions when we have a healthy perspective about ourselves. God desires to see all of His children live a full and liberated life. We live in freedom when we have clarity about our identity in Him. When we take on God's identity we find our purpose, dreams, talents, prosperity, and our best lives!

God-Given Purpose

God made us in His own image; He formed us out of the dust from the ground. He breathed the breath of life into our nostrils, and we became living beings. We are alive because we have a purpose, destiny, and calling. The word, 'purpose' is defined as the thing that God created you to do on earth; it is the reason that you were born. Everything about you, including your race, sex, who your parents are, where you were born, your body type, and your personality traits, were intentionally chosen because these are the factors to help you fulfill your purpose. Your life purpose is the very thing that God assigned you to do before you were conceived.

Growing up in my home church in Decatur, Georgia, my youth leader would always ask me, "What is your purpose?" At the time, I would always get mad at him because I didn't know. The more he asked that question, the more curiosity it sparked in me. Furthermore, the more I began to question it, the more I asked God and sought Him for answers. When I asked God questions about my purpose, they weren't fluffed prayers, but simple questions. My prayers were along the lines of, "What is my purpose? What is my destiny? Why am I here on the earth? What am I supposed to be doing? Where should I start?" Sometimes, we want the full answers to questions in one sitting. I have learned that these questions were being answered throughout the years. Understanding the different levels of my purpose in life was not an overnight process.

I learned more about my purpose in God every year through struggles, questioning, and defining moments. When God revealed some of what He wanted from my life, the timing was perfect! God sent people, dreams, and visions to speak to me about my purpose. Try seeking God through praying, fasting, worshiping, and studying His Word. These spiritual disciplines will allow God to download His passions and desires into your heart.

Once I knew more of my purpose and where I was headed in life, I realized how money played an important role in this pursuit. Moving forward, the decisions I made about my budget, investments, and savings began to correlate with my God-given purpose. I now had a vision for the money God gave me! This direction caused me to invite the wisdom of the Holy Spirit to continue to guide me in making optimal judgments.

There are some things we don't know or don't have because we simply did not ask God. I implore you to ask God what your purpose is and allow your budget to mirror where you are headed in life. Remember, a lady who knows she is called according to His purpose will allow her Creator to be the God over her finances. She chases after her purpose, not money.

God-Given Talents

As God's daughter, He wants you to realize the many gifts and talents He has placed inside of us so that we can do the work we were created to do. Every gift and talent is meant to please Him and bring glory to His name. A talent is a natural ability that you have. It takes you little effort to perform this talent. For example, my cousin can dance very well. Since she was a kid, she's always had the ability to easily catch a beat and stay on beat. As for me, I was rhythmically challenged. I had to work hard to catch a beat and stay on beat. Dancing clearly was not my God-given talent. However, I was a runner, and she was terrible at running. When I accepted that I was not a dancer, but a runner, I went far in life. Although I still had to train and refine my skills, it was natural for me to improve in running. Sometimes we compare ourselves to other people's gifts and talents instead of embracing our own. If I would have spent time taking dance classes to keep up with her, I would have lost myself and caused unnecessary stress in my life. Instead, I had an honest conversation with myself and focused on my God-given talents. I became the top runner at my high school and in the state of Georgia. I went on to college with several scholarship offers, and it provided me with so many opportunities that dancing could not give me.

If you know how to monetize your gift, you can make money from your talents. Furthermore, if you submit your gift back to God, He will allow money and opportunities to flow to you. Submitting your gift to God means that you acknowledge Him every time you use your gift. Giving your gift to God also requires honoring the fact that the gift came from Him. You invite God into your life to help you make the best decisions on using these talents that He has given you. Colossians 3:17 states, "And whatever you do or say, do it as a representative of the Lord Jesus, giving thanks through him to God the Father." As you grow in your gifts and talents, remember to use them as a service to the Lord and allow God to provide for you financially. When you are living out your purpose and using your God-given talents and abilities, money will come to you.

God-Given Goals and Dreams

One of the many ways God speaks to us is through our dreams. God often communicates to us in our dreams because He has a message about the future, or He wants to give us a warning for ourselves or someone else. In addition, because our spirit is alert when we sleep, God will often answer the concerns of our hearts through our dreams. As God downloads dreams to you, your job is to continue to seek God on the timing to pursue that dream. Ask Him to give you a plan about how to achieve the dream that He has given you. When you have a plan, start to create goals or steps to accomplish the big dream. A goal is a strategy developed to reach an expected end.

It is important to share with you that knowing your identity, purpose, talents, and goals does not exempt you from experiencing challenges in life. I want to warn you that chasing your dreams and goals will have obstacles. There will be times when you will struggle in your mind as you pursue this dream. You may get distracted or experience unexpected life events. The list of obstacles can go on and on.

There are going to be challenges that God allows to happen in your life to build resilience and mental fortitude. Resilience and mental fortitude are what you need to be successful in your journey of flourishing financially. You will need to have the fortitude and stamina to make wise decisions when temptations and disappointments take place on your journey. When these God-designed challenges come up, do not fret. God can interrupt your dreams to take you on a path that may take longer than expected, but you will always be where you need to be. There will also be times when your money may not align at the moment with what God is saying. We will dive deeper into having faith and believing in miracles in your money in another chapter. For now, let's look at an example of a God-given dream and how goals were set in place to achieve that dream.

God has given you a dream to be a fashion executive. To start, you want to create a Youtube channel making videos about exclusive fashion pieces. You realize that there will be several things that you need to get started. Your goal is to buy a camera, microphone, laptop, and a few fashion pieces by the end of the year, which is about $2,000. You currently work a part-time job at Chick-Fil-A making $600 a month and your parents give you a $50 allowance every month. You put away $150 to cover expenses such as paying your tithes, getting your nails done, gas for your car, and caring for your dog. The remaining $500 goes into your savings account. You create your budget to fit your goal and you start executing that plan in January. You stick with the plan and you were able to save $2,500 by the end of May. Additionally, you unexpectedly received extra money from your grandparents which allowed you to add to your savings. You were able to get everything you needed and start your channel by the end of the summer. Your channel and videos went viral and you were able to land an internship in New York for the summer after you graduated high school. Because you managed your money and you were faithful to the little you had, God blessed you with more (Matthew 25:23). Remember that your God-given goals and dreams should be reflected in your budget. In the chapters to come, we will go deeper into learning about how to create a budget.

The Tithing Principle

As a young Christian growing up in a Black Apostolic church, tithing was ingrained into my head. The tithing principle is that we give God ten percent of our monetary increase. In the Old Testament, people gave their best offering of livestock and the first fruit from every tree (Nehemiah 10:35-37). When Jesus died on the Cross and became the ultimate sacrifice, we no longer had to sacrifice animals and food. Instead, we offer ten percent of our monetary earnings.

Every Sunday, at church we would read Malachi 3:8-12 before offering. This scripture teaches us about the importance of offering God ten percent of our earnings. I never questioned it. All I knew was that I didn't want to rob God, be cursed, or be disobedient to my mom for not giving to God. Unfortunately, this trained me to give from a place of fear. God did not want me to give Him anything based on fear. The more I sought God, my relationship and knowledge of Him grew deeper. I experienced Him as a perfect Father, loyal friend, place of safety, and sovereign King. I wanted to give Him what He wanted because I honored Him and His commands. Tithing became a form of worship for me. We can worship God through serving His people, giving Him a shout of praise, giving our gifts and talents back to Him, and through our finances. We were made for God and everything that we are and everything that we have belongs to Him (Colossians 1:16). There may be times you struggle financially where the ten percent you owe God through tithing, could be the amount you need to pay a bill. When challenges arise such as this one, remember that tithing is a sacrifice, but ultimately God will take care of us and supply all of our needs according to His glorious riches (Philippians 4:19).

Chapter 1 Bloomanista Reflection Questions

Directions: Take time to ask God and yourself these questions about your identity, purpose, talents, and tithes.

1. What is one incorrect perspective about yourself that did not come from God? Who made you believe these lies?

2. What are some ways you can remind yourself of who you are in Christ daily?

3. Have you asked God what your purpose is? If so, what has God shown you?

4. What are the recurring events, ideas, passions, or desires that you have?

5. What are some things that you are naturally good at?

6. How will you dedicate your gifts and talents back to God?

7. What talents do you need to focus on in this season of your life?

8. Do you struggle with giving God ten percent of your earnings? Why or why not?

9. Why is it important to you to worship God with your finances?

Two

Blossoming into a Giver

Generosity

Generosity is what I like to describe as an altruistic act of kindness that involves a lifestyle of giving. Giving can consist of freely sharing your time, money, wealth, resources, skills, and much more with other people. In this chapter, we will discuss having a cheerful attitude when giving, the principle of reaping and sowing, and giving out of obedience.

Cheerful Giving

God appreciates a cheerful giver. God desires for His daughters to be a giver that doesn't count the cost, moves without hesitation, and worships God through their giving. 2 Corinthians 9:7 states, "You must each decide in your heart how much to give. And don't give reluctantly or in response to pressure. For God loves a person who gives cheerfully." When we give what God has told us to freely share, we should do this with gladness in our hearts.

Imagine going to your parents and asking them for $20. They give it to you, but you know it was not given with a positive attitude. They tell you how many bills they have to pay, mention how you asked them last week for money and they simply give you every reason why they didn't want to give you their money. It made you feel unsettled and annoyed that you even had to ask them for money. Now, imagine God being in your place. He asks you to give $20 to a friend, and you react the same way your parents responded to you in this example. You give Him every reason why you think it's yours, what you were planning to do with it, and how it is all you have left. You gave it to your friend, but you complained to God every second of the way. It's not enough to do what He says, but you must do it with a cheerful attitude. Obey Him without complaining and murmuring (Philippians 2:14). Giving monetarily is only one form of giving. Your time, energy, resources, skills, and talents are other forms of giving that you should also practice cheerfully sharing with people that God sends you to help.

During my time in college, spring breaks for my friends included planning a trip to somewhere sunny and taking a break from the pressure of our studies. I always wanted to go on their seemingly fun trips, but God always called me to go on mission trips with our campus ministry. Instead of drinking, partying, and mingling with the guys, I had to serve. Our service projects consisted of working in food pantries, gardens, orphanages, and other places. God was asking me to give my hands, feet, time, and energy to serve someone else. In hindsight, I see now that God was starting to develop my character and work ethic to keep pushing me more towards a servant-leadership lifestyle. He was also keeping me from a partying lifestyle that could have been disastrous for my destiny. As a college student, I complained, kicked, and screamed because it seemed like everybody else was living the college partying dream. I wanted to do what everyone else was doing. Fortunately, for me, God's vision for my life trumped my youthful ambitions. God saw my future and started to train me about giving early on in my life. Those moments have done more for me now than getting wasted and partying could ever have done for my future.

Nowadays, when God asks me to give my money, time, talent, and service, I know that He is doing something bigger than me. He cultivated inside of me a lifestyle of giving; therefore, I do not wrestle with letting go of the things that He freely gave me. Since I was made to do His will and partner with Him on earth, my attitude has shifted to cheerfully give. In return, I have more joy, peace, and love. Practice freely sharing what God has given you with other people. Ask God to help you develop a lifestyle of joyfully giving.

Sowing and Reaping

Have you ever thought about how rich people stay rich? According to the Econofact Network, Households with more income and wealth are more likely to give any amount and donate more money to good causes.1 From a biblical standpoint, this is what you call sowing and reaping. The principle of sowing and reaping applies to everyone who uses it including Christians and non-Christians. Not only is this a monetary principle, but it also applies to how you treat people. If you sow hatred or a good deed, you will eventually reap what you sowed. For the sake of this book, we will focus solely on this principle from a monetary perspective.

Imagine a farmer preparing to sow seeds for her strawberry farm. She has to pick a spot in the ground that receives a lot of sunlight, prep her soil, and position her water sources. After weeks of cultivating her seeds, she soon receives bountiful baskets of strawberries. Because she sowed or planted hundreds of strawberry seeds on good ground, she reaped thousands of strawberries. She reaped or received back what she sowed, plus more. The following season, she worked just as hard as the previous season but was unable to harvest anything until two seasons later. During the time she waited, she did not stop cultivating the good seed that she planted. When it was time to harvest, she received triple the amount of strawberries from the year before. This example shows us that sometimes God will allow your reaping season to be later than you expected, but it will always be on time! We may not instantly get back what we planted, but if we trust God there is a greater reward waiting for us because of our patience.

I encourage you to give with the mindset of being cheerful and patient. Never stop sowing because ultimately you will reap what you sow. Luke 6:38 declares, "Give, and you will receive. Your gift will return to you in full—pressed down, shaken together to make room for more, running over, and poured into your lap. The amount you give will determine the amount you get back." We serve a generous God that created you to be a daughter that is full of generosity. He wants you to overflow with so many blessings that you have to share them with other people. The more you give in wisdom using the principle of sowing and reaping, the more I believe God will blow on your finances. He will give you abundance so that you can have the means to finance God's vision for the world.

Obedience

I have many anecdotes on how obedience to God stretched my wisdom on handling money in God's way. At the beginning of an unpredictable and unforgettable year, 2020, I decided to follow God by leaving my nice paying job to pursue a different career path. I had a little money saved, but it was not enough to last me beyond a few months. I was simply living on faith and believing God to supply my needs. One day, I was talking to my step-sister when she shared with me that she wanted to host an event for single moms. She desired to build a community around her and exercise some of the creativity she had inside of her. God laid it on my heart to sponsor the space; therefore, I immediately obeyed Him. Although I listened to Him, in my head, I was thinking, "I'm not working, I'm the one that needs a sponsor." After I saw the dent in my account and the bills that I needed to pay, I started to get anxious. After a while, I settled myself and trusted that God would take care of me. Every week I saw blessing after blessing. I received unexpected checks in the mail, friends randomly gave me money without knowing I needed it, my insurance unexpectedly went down, and the volunteer site I worked at gave me food every week. I can go on and on about how God blessed me through one act of obedience.

My step-sister's event got canceled because the facility was closed due to COVID-19. I was able to get back the money I gave to her for the event. I used it later for a well-needed birthday getaway. God showed me some reasons why it was important for me to be obedient about freely sharing that money with my step-sister. I believe that if I would have disobeyed, it would have affected my step-sister's faith in believing God to provide. She was in a place where she was building a deeper relationship with God and learning to trust God with her finances. I also believe that I would have stopped some of the things that God wanted to bless me with.

Sometimes, God will ask you to do something that you do not fully understand at the moment. As a daughter, we must obey our heavenly Father and understand that He's the only One that can see what we can't. He's wiser than we are and He simply knows what is best. Jesus says to the disciples in John 14:15, "If you love me, keep my commandments." Since we serve a sovereign God whose blessings maketh rich and add no sorrow, we can trust and obey God when it comes to our finances (Proverbs 10:22). I encourage you to take the time to pray and ask God to give you a heart that is generous, cheerful, and obedient in spending your finances so that you can experience His continuous blessings.

Chapter 2 Bloomanista Reflection Questions

Directions: Take time to ask God these questions about generosity, sowing and reaping, and obedience.

1. What is one of the biggest reasons you hesitate to be generous?

2. What are some ways you can be generous with your time, money, and talents?

3. What are some things you believe God is challenging you to do to be a better giver?

4. What are some reasons you fail to be obedient to sowing (or being generous)?

Three

Digging to the Root

Emotions Affect Your Habits

In my mid 20's, I became more aware of how my undealt with negative emotions was adversely affecting my body, faith, and choices. I experienced deep internal struggles that often left me severely depressed and worried. Taking care of our emotions and internal pain is important because it determines how we handle stress, relationships, and financial decisions. For me, the struggles with anxiety and depression were very mild at first and appeared once a year. Later it progressed and began to show up often. It affected my career, relationships, and finances. Dealing with internal issues gave me a unique perspective on retail therapy, deeper issues of spending, self-control, guilt after purchases, and recovery from a setback.

Retail Therapy

In 2019, I experienced a high volume of feeling anxious and depression. I was stressed about my living situation, my romantic relationship, friendships, and grad school. At times, it was so hard for me to get out of bed, focus on my job, and be emotionally stable. I felt so disturbed and unsettled on a consistent basis. Because I did not have the language for what was going on at the time, I coped through several unhealthy ways. The top way I coped was through shopping. I shopped, shopped, shopped, and shopped some more! Many people call trying to feel better by shopping, retail therapy. With a lot of disposable income, I shopped to make myself feel better. I would emotionally spend money on food, clothes, and everything I thought that I needed. I was impulsive and shopping became an addiction. It made me feel like I was in control because I couldn't control everything else around me. Later, I shopped myself into debt, and that was when I realized I had deeper issues that needed to be resolved.

I would feel great the moment that I bought items that I enjoyed. There can be benefits from retail therapy, but ultimately you want to discover your true purpose in making purchases. Asking deeper questions and being honest about specific purchases will help you understand your true self. Being thoughtful about your behaviors can help you grab hold of addictions early so you can be your best self and make wiser decisions with what God blesses you with in the future. In the end, He will bless you with more when you learn how to manage the little that you already have in your possession (Luke 16:10).

If we are not careful, we can ignore our real issues if we continue to use retail therapy to hide behind our problems. Ultimately, we can use many activities to make ourselves feel better. These devices will work for the moment, but the only source of true, long-lasting joy comes from God.

Deeper Issues of Spending

The spiritual and emotional problems that I faced showed up through impulsive buying, emotional spending, and control issues. These abysmal outward actions caused me to seek God and counseling. I confronted these broken areas in my life and God showed me the root causes of my issues. In the end, I made healthier financial decisions. Take a self-assessment on what your terrible spending habits are trying to tell you about your deep internal struggles. Here are some examples of issues that can appear in your finances.

Rejection- Sometimes we make poor economic choices because of an internal battle called rejection. This example highlights what we can get caught up in if we do not heal from rejection. One time a group of people planned a trip, and a certain person wasn't invited. Out of retaliation against the group, that certain person planned a trip without inviting them. The trip ended up being very expensive, a lot went wrong, and they did not have a good time. The crazy part is the other group didn't end up going on their trip so this certain person was stuck with a trip that shouldn't have happened because of undealt with rejection issues. Sometimes we spend money because we feel rejected. Instead of giving those issues to God, we look for ways to make ourselves feel better, and it ends up putting a hole in our pocket. Many examples reveal deeper issues of why we spend so we must be honest with ourselves and allow God to heal that area of our life.

Attention Seeking- Some of us spend money because we have been rejected and want someone to take notice of us. This example delineates the thought process of actions that take place that cause us to act out of character with our finances. While scrolling through Instagram, a guy you saw and liked is a chef. With ulterior motives, you reach out to him showing interest in his meal prepping service. You knew you barely had the funds to purchase his service, but you decided you wanted his attention. You got his attention, and it left you broke! Come to find out, he had a girlfriend. You wasted time, money, and energy. Wanting attention from him was a deeper issue that God had to handle. The more you realize how much you do for attention, the more you will stop seeking attention and save a lot more money!

Media Influence- Every day we see something on social media that we think looks better than what we currently have in our lives. We begin to compare ourselves to others and strive for a life that was never intended to be ours. At times, we make financial decisions to post online to make it appear to others that "we got it, too." This mindset will leave you impoverished. You must be content with what you have and be careful to not let outside influences dictate what you buy. Remember that your money belongs to God.

Poor Body Image- A friend you once knew hated the way she looked. She spent thousands of dollars a year to buy lash extensions, hair extensions, make-up, nails, teeth, and implants. As she grew in her relationship with Christ, the more she accepted how God made her physically. She saved so much money a year when she got to the deeper issue of why she didn't like her body.

Acceptance- Your sister shares an experience with you where she spent a lot of money for acceptance. She felt the more she bought for this guy she was dating, the more he would love her. When she matured, she realized that she didn't have to buy her way into anything. She acknowledged that love didn't cost a thing. If he didn't love her for her, he didn't need to be in her life. Your sister soon applied this to every friendship and romantic relationship in her life and found true happiness. She also saved a lot of money by getting to the deeper issues of why she was spending so much in that relationship. It was life-changing!

If any of the examples or inner battles resonated with you, then seek help to heal from rejection, people-pleasing, comparison, self-hatred, and so on. What you spend your money on, reveals a lot about what is going on inside of you. Therapy, counseling, praying, fasting, and other spiritual disciplines can help you on your journey of healing.

Self-Control

One of the biggest keys to flourishing in your finances is having self-control. In Galatians 5:22-23, Paul lists the fruits of the spirit such as love, peace, joy, patience, kindness, goodness, faithfulness, gentleness, and self-control. God gave us His Spirit when we accepted Him as our Savior. Because we are not perfect, we have to develop in these areas that Paul lists in Galatians 5. Walking in the spirit will lead us to an abundant life. When we walk in the spirit, this means that we do not gratify our lustful desires whenever we please. As godly women, we must continue to exercise discipline and self-control so that we can make successful financial decisions.

Delayed gratification is the perfect way to grow in self-control and discipline. A mentor once shared a story of how he had children learn about the importance of not always gratifying their first desires. He shared with us that he gave students candy at the beginning of his class. By the end of class, he checked to see who ate their candy. For the students who did not eat their candy, he gave them extra at the end. This story was to allow students to understand that we can have better outcomes in life when we choose to be patient. As adults, if we act on every desire that comes up, we will continue to make horrible decisions with our money. Teaching ourselves to wait will not only help us excel in our finances, but it will help in other areas of our lives. Waiting helps you to think more about what you want to purchase and be less impulsive. I encourage you to practice self-control, delayed gratification, and walk in the spirit when it comes to your finances.

Progress and Not Perfection

As you begin to journey towards gaining control over your finances, you will have setbacks. Learning new habits takes time, and you will fail at some of your goals. The good thing is God will always use your setbacks as a learning opportunity. The devil is committed to making you fail just as much as God is committed to you flourishing in your finances. When you have weak moments, the enemy will condemn you. The enemy will make you feel like you'll never get it right. This is a lie. I hope that you do not feed into it. When you fall, get back up and ask God for more wisdom and self-control in this area. If you realize that you need help in gaining control of your mental health, emotions, spiritual struggles, and internal bruises, you may want to consult a mentor, therapist, or counselor to get to the core issues. Remember progress and not perfection!

Chapter 3 Bloomanista Reflection Questions

Directions: Take time to ask God these questions about unhealthy spending habits.

1. Have I ever noticed that when I am feeling down mentally or emotionally my spending habits change for better or worse?

2. Instead of looking for material ways to solve my issues, how can I give my burdens to God and pursue wholeness?

3. How can I practice the fruits of the spirit, especially self-control, when it comes to my finances?

4. Can I identify with any of the given examples concerning deeper issues of spending?

5. While on my financial journey, what are some ways that I can remind myself of the little victories instead of focusing on being perfect?

Four

Thriving in Faith

Imagine being in your home and wanting something to eat. You failed to go grocery shopping and you weren't up for the journey to leave your warm cozy house to drive in five inches of snow to the store. You go into your kitchen believing that you will find something to make a meal. You look in your cabinets and fridge where you find two random items. With these items, you decide to make a meal. After cooking this food, you weren't hungry anymore, and you began to make this meal all the time. You love making this meal because you know that it works! There are spiritual ingredients that you need to use to make your journey to flourishing in your finances work. Prayer and faith are going to be the key components to seeing miraculous things happen in your finances. This money recipe is one of God's favorite meals to receive from His children, and it never fails! If you are nervous about where money will come from, this chapter will unlock some of the key things that you will need to grow in your faith in God. Let's explore more about prayer, faith, and miracles related to helping you in this learning experience.

Prayer

How many things do you not have because you simply did not ask your parents, teachers, or friends? How many things do you not have because you didn't ask your Heavenly Father? "You have not because you ask not" is a scripture in James 4:2 that is simple, but powerful. As a daughter of God, He wants you to know that you can come to Him to ask Him for anything. He's not like our earthly father; God is a perfect Father. He knows you completely because He made you, and He never wants you to hide from Him. You can be bold and confident when you come to Him in prayer, and ask for what you need.

Prayer is simply having communication with God. You can talk to Him like you are talking to another human. You don't have to clean yourself up spiritually before you talk to Him, nor do you have to have this long, drawn-out process of trying to connect with Him. A prayer can be undecorated and straightforward. There are times when I journal my prayers, color scripture pages, go on a walk, go for a drive, or bend on my knees by my bed to pray. Those ways work for me, but it's up to you to find out your unique way of talking to God. The great part about being connected to God is that He hears the cries of your heart. He knows exactly what you need before you say anything. Your job is to pray without ceasing according to 1 Thessalonians 5:17. You are to trust that He hears you when you pray. Prayer is an essential part of every area of your life including your finances. God wants to lead you in this area of your life. He leads you by way of your prayers or daily communication with Him.

When I was in middle school, my mom and dad divorced. Before she got remarried to my stepdad in high school, she was single. It was just her and me. She did her best to provide for me. Understanding that she barely had enough to support me, I knew she wouldn't have the funds for me to go to college. I was an excellent track and cross country runner with phenomenal coaches. I prayed all the time to God that He would provide opportunities for me to run on a collegiate level. I made my ask to God specific, and I believed He was listening to me. Philippians 4:6 states, "Do not worry about anything, but in everything by prayer and supplication with thanksgiving let your requests be made known to God. And the peace of God, which surpasses all understanding, will guard your hearts and your minds in Christ Jesus." I didn't worry or fear about my plans to become a runner in college. I prayed and believed which was what kept me peaceful. After four years of praying and working hard, I received several scholarships. My mom barely had to pay for school, and God provided!

Prayer will be a vital part of God giving you financial blessings. Sometimes it will take time for your prayers to be answered, but God's timing is perfect. Occasionally, you may not get exactly what you want, but you must trust that God knows what's best for you. If God hasn't allowed something to happen, it's either because the timing wasn't right, it wasn't good for you, or other reasons you may not understand until years later. He's protective and you can trust Him to take care of you.

Faith

Faith is having a belief in someone or something. For example, when you sit in a chair, you believe it will support you. You confidently put your weight and expectations in this chair hoping the legs will not break. Our prayer life should look the same! You must have faith when you communicate with God by putting all of your hope in Him. God was so eager for you to come to Him that He allowed Jesus to die to give you full access to communicating with God. He wants you to come to Him with great joy and anticipation!

As a young college graduate, I moved to Chicago to pursue a career in the nonprofit sector. I was supported by two service programs. Once they ended, I felt the call to stay in Chicago. I didn't have a place to live or a job, and I wanted to go to graduate school to get a master's degree. I had enough faith to believe that everything I needed God would supply because I knew that He wanted me to stay in Chicago. I prayed with faith. In addition, I moved with the expectation that God would answer my heart's desires by applying for jobs and searching for housing. God provided me with a salary job in my field and an affordable studio apartment. I furnished my house for little to nothing. I got a part-time night job working at a restaurant so I could have a few extra dollars. The restaurant provided free meals for employees which cut down on grocery expenses, and my full-time job gave me a lot of other discounts that helped cut down on expenses. It wasn't necessarily how I wanted to live, but I had everything I needed. I was fully content. After a year of trusting God to supply for me, He provided me with a job that doubled my current salary. I paid all of my bills, saved money, got another apartment of my dreams, the car of my dreams, and paid for graduate school out of pocket. God provided me with everything I needed, and I lacked nothing! According to 1 Corinthians 5:7, Paul states, "We live by faith, not by sight." In the beginning, I didn't see how it was going to happen, but I trusted that God heard my prayers. I had the faith to believe that He would take care of me financially. I believe that if I would have made a decision not to follow God but only trust what I saw, I would have missed out on what He had for me. I encourage you to be a lady who uses the recipe of faith-based prayers. Believe God for it, rest in His promises for your life, and watch Him work!

Miracles

When people think about miracles, they consider God using His supernatural abilities to make something happen that cannot be explained by humans. Miracles often leave people in awe and wonder of the power of God. While on earth, Jesus performed miraculous faith healings, exorcisms, resurrections, and control over nature. It is great to know that we have access to this power. Jesus is still performing miracles today!

In 2020, I was not working, and I decided to switch career paths. During this time, I was totally dependent on God to supply my needs. There were times when my bank account was in the negatives; I had cents to my name and a lot of debt. Every month, God provided for me in miraculous ways. There were times when I received rebates, settlement checks from my old jobs, discounts, tax returns, stimulus checks, monetary gifts from family members, and so many other forms of income. One time, I experienced a financial miracle. At this specific moment, I noticed that I had just enough money in my account to pay my car note. Once that money would be taken out, I was going to have nothing left in my account. That night, I prayed to God and worshiped Him as He forced me to trust Him through this ongoing process of building my faith. In the middle of prayer and worship, I focused on who God is and what His word says about Him. After that night of worshiping and believing in God, I noticed that my car note wasn't taken out of my account. I called to see if something was wrong and the employee said, "We received your payment ma'am." I said, "How? The money is still in my account." The employee said, "On our end, it shows that we received your payment on this date." At that moment, I realized God's amazing, miraculous power. He showed me that He's the God over the computer systems and accounts. I learned that when I put Him first in my finances and trust Him, He will supply for me. What seems impossible to us is easy for Him.

During this season of having little, I was honest. I continued to pay my tithes with the little that came in, made sure I paid my bills, and I didn't rely on my parents for money. God rewarded me for being faithful and content with the little. I never missed a meal or any bill payments. It was hard and an emotional rollercoaster to believe at times, but He was always faithful. One of my favorite scriptures is 1 Timothy 6:6 which simply states that Godliness + contentment= Great Gain. I followed God, I was content with where He had me in life, and He gave me much more than what I felt I lost.

The money recipe is having faith when you ask God for what you need financially. Our faith should not be shaken when we find ourselves with little. Our perspective about God should not be tainted when we do not have the money we think we should have in our possession. Focus on the nature of God so that He can increase your faith. Bring all of your needs to Him, and He will give you peace to be content in whatever financial season that you are in. I encourage you to rest in His sovereignty and believe that He has it already worked out. I believe and pray that God will show you His miraculous ways when you allow Him to lead you in your finances.

Chapter 4 Bloomanista Reflection Questions

Directions: Take time to ask God these questions about prayer, faith, and miracles.

Do parts of my prayer life involve asking God to meet my financial needs? If not, how can I start communicating to God about what I need financially?

In what ways can you prevent fear and doubt from taking over your thought life?

What are some things you would like to believe God for in the area of your finances?

Take a moment to think about how God provided financial miracles for you and your family in the past. Based on that knowledge, how can you believe in Him for more starting today?

Five

Preparing to be Alert

The Love of Money Is The Root Of All Evil

Money, wealth, and resources are God-given creations that were placed on the earth. Unfortunately, the love of money has perverted why it was originally created. Today, in a lot of cases, you will find that the center of conflict, division, or war is probably money. Without a godly perspective on money, you will find yourself doing things that are out of character. Because money is the root of all evil, in this chapter I want to briefly show you how to be aware of fraudulent activity concerning your finances.

Scammers

In my 20's, when I first moved out on my own and I was getting the hang of being an adult, it felt like scammers had a radar on my back. I was barely making any money, but I would find myself in situations where scammers sold me on phrases like, "saving money on my bills," "making extra cash a week," and "you have to buy now." Luckily, I stopped a lot of the scams before they had a significant impact on me. When something didn't feel right, I asked my mentors, friends, and family members about it. Also, those gut feelings were the Holy Spirit sending alerts to me to pay attention to the scams.

Scammers work day and night to get every dollar you may have in your possession. They will appear very legit and innocent, but their main goal is to get rich off of other people's money. According to the Better Business Bureau, people from the age of 18-34 are most likely to get scammed. 1 It has been said that 70% of consumers in the US are women. Marketing strategies are designed to appeal to women because women are more likely to buy than men. As a young lady with a godly perspective on money, your job is to use wisdom from the Holy Spirit in your spending. Your job is to be alert, but do not fear. Anything that makes you feel like you have to rush to make a decision is probably not from God. If you become sensitive to the Holy Spirit, He will always lead you, stop you, and warn you.

Things to look out for:

Random links or emails that come to your phone

- A random check comes in the mail without you signing up for anything
- Someone asking for your social security number, login information, account number, or personal information
- A message saying "There's suspicious activity on your account, please login here."
- Business people on the street pressuring you to sign up for something
- Contest and drawings
- You have to buy now or the deal will expire in 24 hours
- Scammers posing to be well-known companies
- Random phone calls that pose as an emergency and prompt you to press a number

What to ask before you buy.

- Is this something I really need?
- Do I feel rushed to make a decision?
- Can I afford this, or can it wait?
- Did I do my research on this product?
- Is this company legit?

These are a few examples but remember, if it sounds too good to be true, then it probably is. Do your research before you buy certain products, and read the fine print!

Financial Freedom

Being a slave to debt is not of God! It is God's desire that we live financially free. Being financially free is being financially stable. Being financially stable means that we do not slave for money. We get to use money as a tool to make our dreams and other people's dreams come true. When people are financially free they can save and make wise investments to multiply their money. God has called us to live freely and abundantly in our mind, soul, life, and finances. Jesus lived a simple lifestyle and did not have a lot of things. He didn't owe people anything and He wasn't concerned with the latest things on the market. Every resource that He had, He used the Holy Spirit to guide Him in how to use it. As daughters of a great Father, future leaders, mothers, and business owners, working towards financial freedom will be a key component to how well you are able to do what God has called you to do.

Chapter 5 Bloomanista Reflection Questions

Directions: Take time to answer these questions with God about how you can become more alert on your journey of financial freedom.

1. What are some ways I can change my mindset to be on a path to becoming financially free?

2. What can I intentionally do to protect my assets?

3. What are ways I can ensure that my heart doesn't become a lover of money, but my perspective stays on God?

Six

A Bloomanista's Budget

A budget is a set amount of money you allocate (set aside) towards expenses. Creating a budget means that you have a plan for your money every single day. People with a budget, think about what they can or cannot afford. Budgeting allows you to bring order to your finances and stay focused on your God-given goals. As life happens, your budget will change, but it is imperative that you practice as a teenager or young adult, how to budget your money. In essence, each dollar you have should have an assignment or placement. Plan in advance where your money will go. When money is not assigned to a specific category in your life, you will find yourself spending without a keen perspective on priority. In this chapter, I will show you how to create a budget that will reflect your God-given goals!

Creating a Budget

Phase One Budget Worksheet

Directions: The first step in creating a budget is understanding your long-term and short-term goals. Refer to the example below to list all of your long-term and short-term goals in the blank chart provided.

Example

What are your long-term goals? (6 months- 1 year)	In the next 6 months, I want to have: $600 saved towards getting a car $450 saved towards taking a summer trip $400 saved towards my prom dress
What are your short-term goals? (3 months)	In the next 3 months, I want to have half o my long-term goals met: $300 saved towards getting a car $150 saved towards taking a summer trip $200 saved towards my prom dress

What are your long term goals? (6 months-1 year)	What are your short term goals? (3 months)

Phase Two Budget Worksheet

Directions: Using the chart below, list your weekly, biweekly and monthly income.

Example

I bring home $160 weekly, $320 biweekly, and $640 every month.

Directions: Fill in the blank answering the statements below.

I make________________________every week.

I make________________________biweekly. (Multiply your weekly income by two)

I make ________________________every month. (Multiply your biweekly income by two)

Directions: List your monthly expenses and organize your expenses by importance using the color key.

My Monthly Expenses:

Tithes $64	**Car Fund $100**
Offering $20	**Summer Trip $52**
Phone Bill $72	**Prom Dress $72**
Bus Fare $60	**Extra $200 (Entertainment- Hair, nails, movies, mall, etc.)**

List your monthly expenses.	**Organize your expenses by importance using the color key.** Most Important-Top priority every month. Important- Related to long-term and short-term goals. Less Important-You can live without.

Phase Three Budget Worksheet

Directions: Write out in detail what you spend money on every month. Write your total at the top.

Example

Monthly Budget Total <u>$640</u>
Tithes $64 Offering $20 Phone Bill $72 Bus Fare $60 Car Fund $100 Summer Trip $52 Prom Dress $72 Extra $200 (Entertainment-Hair, nails, movies, mall, etc.)

Monthly Budget Total $_______
List below all of the items that you are responsible for each month.

Directions: In the next section, you will write out your total for your biweekly budget. Refer to the example below to create your own biweekly budget list. *Using your monthly budget, divide each number by two to create your biweekly budget.

Example

Biweekly Budget Total $360
Tithes - $32 Offering - $10 Phone Bill - $36 Bus Fare - $30 Car Fund - $50 Summer Trip - $26 Prom Dress - $36 Extra - $100 (Entertainment-Hair, nails, movies, mall, etc.)

Biweekly Budget Total $_______
List below all of the items you are responsible for biweekly.

Directions: Read the example below to determine your weekly budget. *Using your biweekly expenses, divide each number by two to create your weekly budget. Place your answers in the blank chart below.

Example

Weekly Budget Total $160
Tithes - $16 Offering - $5 Phone Bill - $18 Bus Fare - $15 Car Fund - $25 Summer Trip - $13 Prom Dress - $18 Extra - $50 (Entertainment-Hair, nails, movies, mall, etc.)

Weekly Budget Total $_______
List below all of the items you are responsible for weekly.

***Optional last step. If you want to see how the entire budget works together, use this chart below to combine your weekly, biweekly, and monthly budgets.

Example: Your budget should look similar to this when you are finished.

Weekly $160	**Biweekly $360**	**Monthly $640**
Tithes - $16 Offering - $5 Phone Bill - $18 Bus Fare - $15 Car Fund - $25 Summer Trip - $13 Prom Dress - $18 Extra - $50 (Entertainment-Hair, nails, movies, mall, etc.)	Tithes - $32 Offering - $10 Phone Bill - $36 Bus Fare - $30 Car Fund - $50 Summer Trip - $26 Prom Dress - $36 Extra - $100 (Entertainment-Hair, nails, movies, mall, etc.)	Tithes $64 Offering $20 Phone Bill $72 Bus Fare $60 Car Fund $100 Summer Trip $52 Prom Dress $72 Extra - $200 (Entertainment-Hair, nails, movies, mall, etc.)

Directions: Use this chart below to map out all of your weekly, biweekly, and monthly expenses. This is your official budget!

Weekly $_______	**Biweekly $_______**	**Monthly $_______**

Other Tips

- **Budget Holidays**- If you know Christmas or someone's birthday is coming up and you want to get your family gifts, put them in your budget a couple of months before so you won't be caught off guard.

- **Budgeting Tools**-This is an example of how budgeting will look on paper. Some may find budgeting apps, spreadsheets, and envelopes helpful.

- **Use This Template**- If you have a group that you lead or a business that you have, you can use this same template to budget the finances for those groups or businesses.

- **Be Patient**- It takes time to reach your goals. As long as you discipline yourself and be consistent, you will reach your goals before you know it. You will always be on your way to creating generational wealth and responsibility.

- **Don't Forget Your Little One**- If you have a child, a sibling, or a pet that you take care of, don't forget to include their expenses in your budget.

- **Allow Grace**-You will make mistakes and that's okay. God is the only one that's perfect. Your job is to learn from your mistakes and get back up to try again.

- **Be Positive**- Watch what you say and think! Death and life are in the power of your tongue and you shall eat the fruit thereof. Money may look a little funny at times, but remember how you speak about your money. Even on your worst days, what you say can determine what happens in the future. Having a growth mindset and saying things like, "I had a bad week with not sticking to my budget but I am learning, growing and I will get better."

- **Repeat-** Revisit your budget every three months or as often as you need to check your progress or to make adjustments due to life changes.

- **Give Each Dollar A Job-** Every dollar in your budget should have an assignment. If your money doesn't have an assignment, you could easily get into the habit of just spending.

Seven

Blooming Through Prayer

As you go on your journey, of becoming a "Bloomanista" take these prayers with you. Read each prayer and come in agreement with them for your life by reading them out loud, and saying, Amen! Make these prayers personal by adding your name to them. I hope that through studying finances and praying to God, you allow God to change your perspective about money. I pray that He gives you a godly view on how to flourish with your finances.

Prayers for Bloomanistas

God, I thank You for your daughters and the many ways that you plan to use them in the future to bring out Your will on earth. As they continue to grow in you, I pray that you secure their identity so that they can fully walk in their purpose. Send them people that will affirm their God-given talents and help push them into their destiny. I pray for divine connections and a heart to serve You. As their Father, help them to look for you in every area of their life and be filled up with your love. God let Your will be done in our lives for Your glory. In Jesus' name, Amen.

Dear Heavenly Father, I thank You that You are a God that makes our burdens light. We can find rest in Your sovereignty and be confident that You can be trusted to keep Your promises. I pray that You help Your daughters to become women that don't look for peace and joy outside of You through materialistic things and hide behind any insecurities or lies. Reveal every stronghold and may they be reminded to look for You to mend their broken pieces. Help them to come boldly to the throne of grace and find sweet rest. As You restore any brokenness, let them be reminded of Your goodness, power, and the small victories You give daily. Give them the strength, wisdom, and power to walk in Your spirit in Jesus' name, Amen!

Dear Father, my prayer is that Your daughters may know You as Jehovah-Jireh (a provider). I pray that when they come to You in prayer, that they are not filled with anxiety, they tell you what they need, thank You for what You have already done, and expect Your peace that surpasses all understanding. I pray that they are reminded that You hold all power in Your hands, and in return, their faith rises to believe You for things that they cannot see. Blow their mind with miracles and help them to share the testimonies of how You provided. Let their foundation be firm and their trust be solely in You, in Jesus' name, Amen!

Dear God, I pray that you protect Your daughter's heart from being consumed by the love of money. Help them to be honest with how they receive money. Remind them that You are Lord over everything and their dependence should solely be on You. Protect them from the wiles of the enemy concerning their finances. Help them to be patient in making financial decisions and seek discernment. Shut down every operation that is not like You and bring order to their finances. Give Your daughters wisdom in this area of their life so that it may bring glory to your name in Jesus' name, Amen!

Notes

Chapter 2

Priday, Benjamin, et al. "Are Rich People Really Less Generous?" *Econofact*, 5 May 2020, https://econofact.org/are-rich-people-really-less-generous.

Chapter 5

Better Business Bureau. "BBB Risk Report: Adults 18-24 Were Highest Scam Risk in 2020." *BBB*, 1 Mar. 2021, https://www.bbb.org/article/news-releases/23820-adults-18-24-report-highest-scam-risk-in-2020.

About the Author

Gerlisa D. Shipman

Gerlisa D. Shipman is a Metro Atlanta native whose life mission is to serve through leadership. She graduated from Chowan University with a degree in Psychology/Counseling. Throughout her college career, she started the university's first online publication, and she was the first Black female student government association president.

After graduating in 2015, Gerlisa moved to Chicago where she found a deep love for social justice. She worked for several nonprofit organizations building a volunteer program, organizing around education policy, and working with youth networks on the westside of Chicago.

In 2020, Gerlisa accepted the call to come back home to Georgia and pursue teaching and entrepreneurship. She is currently an elementary school teacher in Metro Atlanta and the CEO and Founder of Efflorescence Girls, LLC. Efflorescence Girls, LLC is a faith-based organization designed to mentor teenage girls and young adult women to have a Godly perspective on, identity, relationships, mental health, self-love, life goals, and financial literacy. Gerlisa plans to continue to innovate through servant leadership in various capacities and live out her mantra which is, “Go Be Great!”

Made in the USA
Monee, IL
04 November 2026

67380874R00036